ILLUSTRATIONS BY LUCY POLLARD

JERICO MANDYBUR

Love Oracle

DIVINE GUIDANCE FOR RELATIONSHIPS

quadrille

For small
creatures such
as we,
the vastness
is bearable
only through love.

CARL SAGAN

How To Use
The Love Oracle

Hold this book to your heart. Relax as you inhale and exhale for three counts.

Quiet your mind and focus on a thoughtful question about love. Feel it radiate in your heart.

Run your fingers along the page edges and, when you feel called, stop and open the book on that page. This is the Goddess of Love's answer to you.

Gently consider how what you've read relates to your situation right now. Journal or reflect on this.

You've Got The Love

Martin Luther King Jr. once said 'I have decided to stick with love, for I know that love is ultimately the only answer to mankind's problems ... Hate is too great a burden to bear.' Acknowledging that even in 1967, talking about love was considered 'emotional bosh', he defined love as a 'strong, demanding' force. One capable of 'pulling down mountains' and 'unlocking the meaning of ultimate reality'.

So often we think of love as a state of infatuation, or a romantic flutter felt between two people in private. But as King affirms – echoed by an infinite number of brilliant minds and hearts across the ages – love is a cosmic energy much bigger, much braver and more world-changing than we can even imagine. And wonderfully, love is our natural state. We come into this world as loving, joyful beings with a great need for each other. As social animals, love is our first and common language.

This oracle is designed to remind you of this natural state. To empower you to give love, receive love, and reflect on all the myriad ways love might allow you to live a full, congruent, expressive and fulfilled life. Use this book to receive answers from the Goddess of Love (or your loving higher power of another name) and let those answers inspire you to grow and attract all the love you seek. Because it's seeking you too.

What kinds of questions can you ask the *Love Oracle*? Any and all thoughtful questions about your life, loves and the wider world. After all, the energy of love is deeply entrenched in not just your sex life and romantic relationships, but in your family life, your friendships, your work, your creative life, your political life and your hopes and dreams for yourself and others. When asking a question of the *Love Oracle*, slow down and get present with your heart space. Remember, the *Love Oracle* presents you with insight, but your emotional inner self holds the key to interpretation. Trust that each answer you receive is perfect for the moment in which it arrives. Some insights are blunt, some need time to digest, and all are lovingly channelled from my heart to yours in the spirit of empowerment and liberation.

I pray your feelings, thoughts and actions bring you closer to the endless fount of love inside you, all around you and to the love you deserve to receive.

WITH LOVE,

JERICO MANDYBUR XO

Symbols
In
Love Oracle

Each slice of wisdom offered in
Love Oracle has been organised
symbolically, according to its
essence. You'll find these
symbols on each page.

Channelled insights to
reflect and meditate on.

Pieces of actionable advice.

Messages from the collective
consciousness a.k.a quotations.

Commit to the daily practice of full-bodied self-acceptance.

How well do you know your turn-ons? Start there.

To heal,
we first have
to give ourselves
full permission
to *feel*.

To give and
to receive love
in proportion
is the measure
of mutuality.

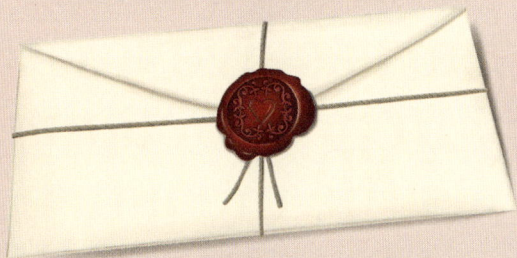

NO ONE'S A
MIND-READER.

Exalt the
sweetness
of a new
connection
being formed.

The more you understand your own shadow, the more compassion you'll feel for others.

'Put yourself
in the way
of beauty.'

CHERYL STRAYED

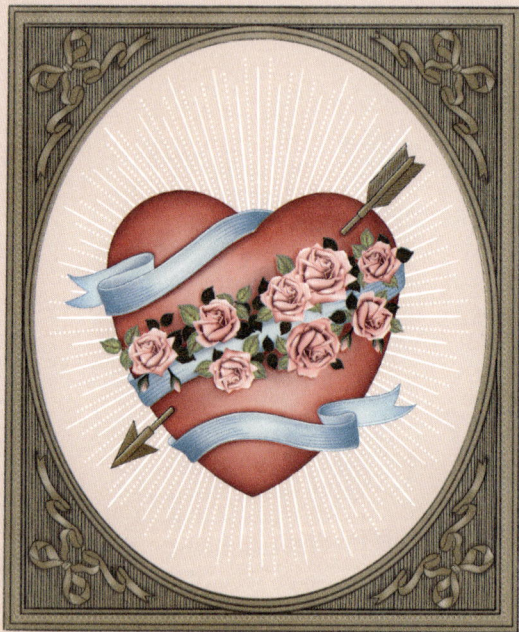

NOTHING
IS SO SOLID.
BE FLEXIBLE.

Savour the gift of experience.

No one is coming
to save you.
Save yourself.

You're allowed
to shower
yourself with
unconditional
adoration.

YOU KNOW
YOU BEST.

Actively disengage
with people whose
actions would
have you doubt
your goodness.

Who lied
to you about
Original Sin?
Empowerment
is not immoral.

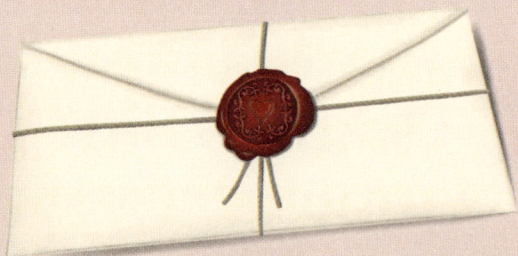

THE ONLY WAY OUT IS THROUGH.

Commit to your enjoyment, even (especially) in dark times.

Rose buds
forced open
will only
be destroyed.

WHO SAID
YOU WEREN'T
WORTH IT?

Divest from performativity by getting out of your head.

ARGUING
A POINT
CAN BE HOT.

'God loves
each of us
as if there
were only
one of us.'

SAINT AUGUSTINE

Dedicate sacred space to cultivating what's on your heart.

Even when
it's scary,
love feels like
a full-bodied 'yes'.

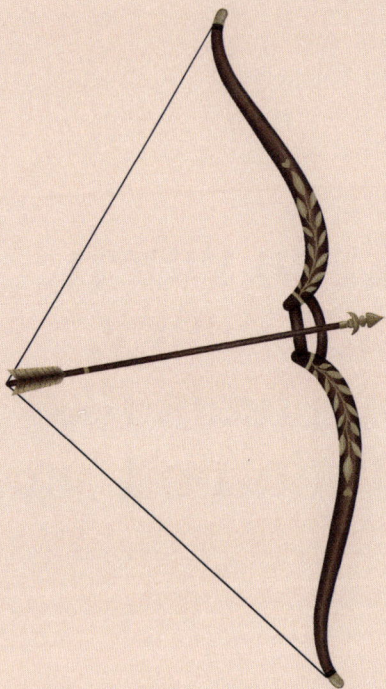

Love is not a finite resource. It's an eternal reality.

WHO BENEFITS FROM YOUR SHAME?

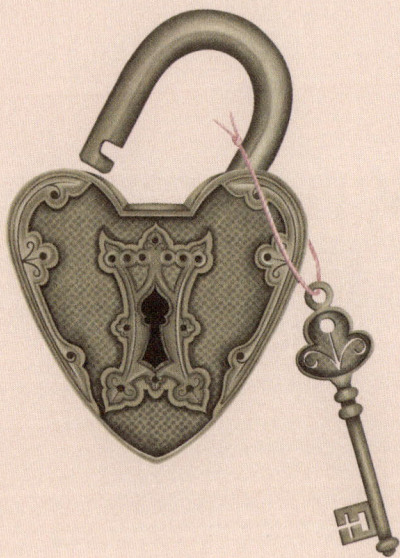

It's safe to acknowledge what your heart wants.

You can change the narrative.

Take a long,
nourishing breath
in through
your nose. Hold.
Now breathe it
out slowly in a full,
rich exhalation.
Repeat for a few
more rounds.

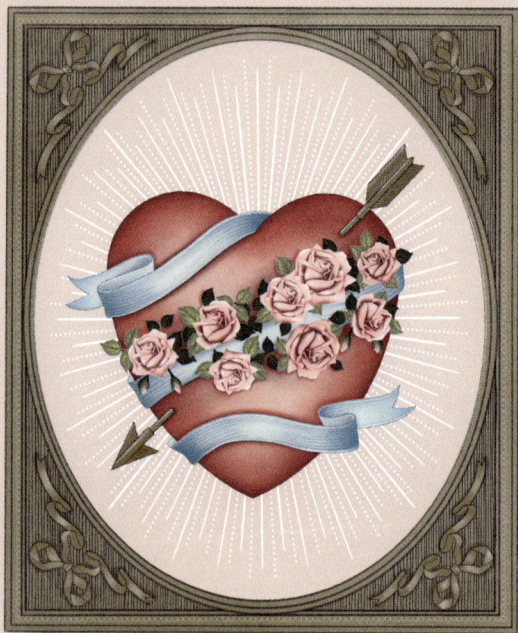

Love is like fire:
when we fuel
it with our
frequent attention,
it gets stronger.

Grief is love at its fullest, deepest expression.

REWRITE YOUR OWN STORY.

What part of you
are your emotional
reactions trying
to take care of?

Deep listening
is the art of loving
someone without
expectations
or demands.

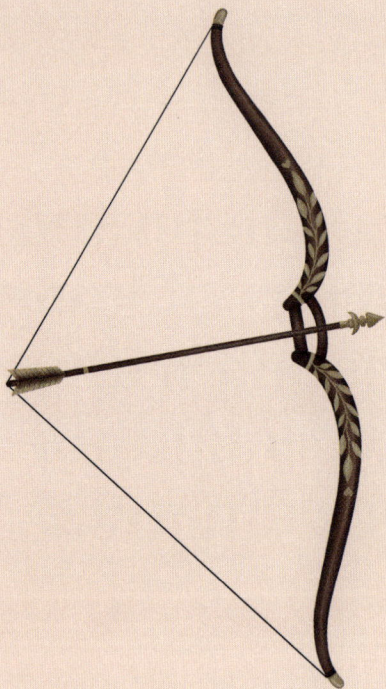

Risk may contain
injury, but it also
contains every
imaginable treasure.

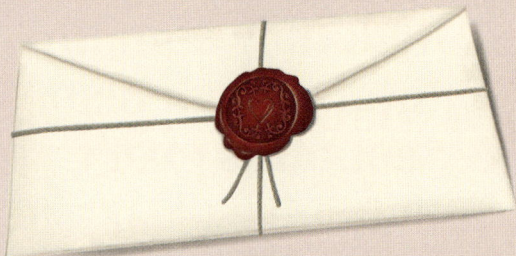

WORDS
HOLD
POWER.

'Have enough courage to trust love one more time and always one more time.'

MAYA ANGELOU

It's not a crime
to experience
unbridled joy.

We love
imperfectly.
That's what
makes it
so sweet.

Love is the only thing that can set us free.

What's your most luxurious, provocative fantasy? Imagine through a story, a playlist, or a dream.

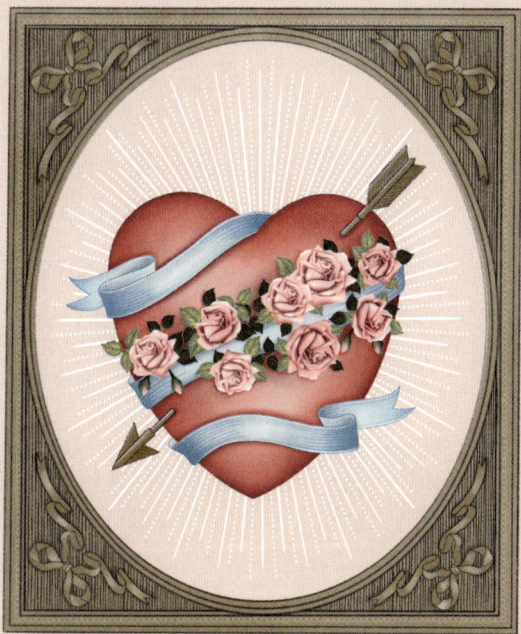

It's hard to hear your heart speak when your mind and body are exhausted.

STAY FIRM IN YOUR TRUTH.

Reacquaint yourself with unhurried, mindful touching.

Your heart has already learned valuable lessons. Treasure them like precious stones.

LOVE CANNOT LIVE WITHOUT TRUST.

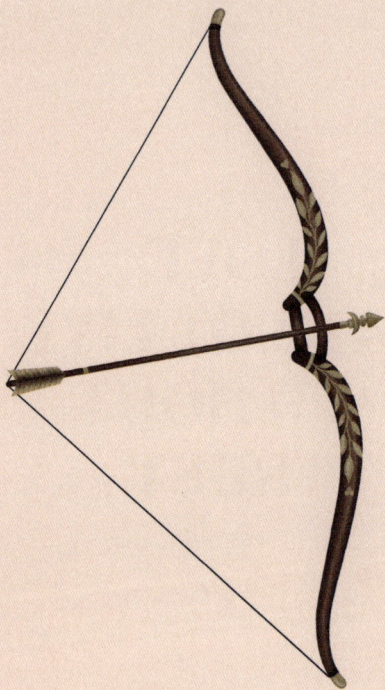

You're already
liberated by love.
You just have
to realise it.

Who says self-love is any less exquisite?

Love is your
evolutionary
instinct. Don't
be afraid to
express it.

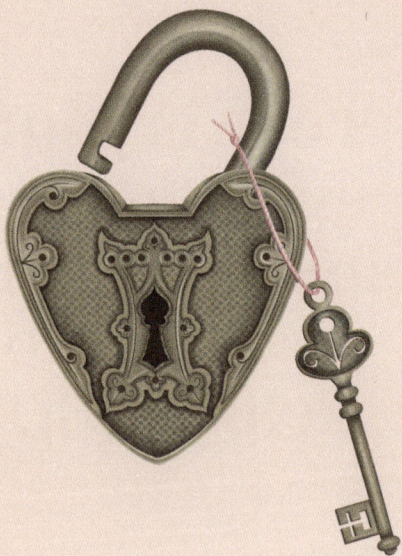

Human connection is as necessary as oxygen.

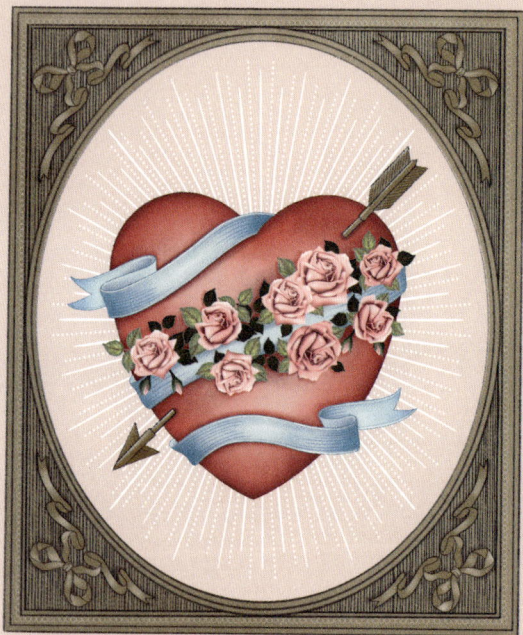

MEET THEM
HALFWAY.

**Practise
reparenting
yourself with
unconditional
positive regard.**

Love doesn't exist in a vacuum. In the material world, it looks like solidarity.

Metabolising
the poison of old
relationships,
stories and
ideas is hard,
necessary work.

Let your
heart beat and
your breath
ground you
in the loving
present moment.

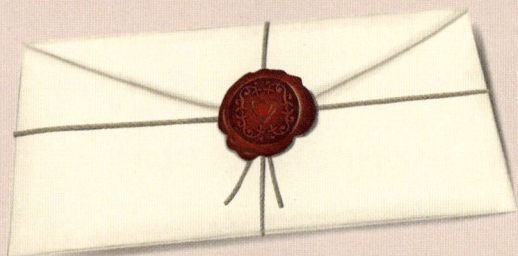

LET IT GO.
LET IT GO.
LET IT GO.

To be present
is to completely
connect with
someone else
in the moment.
Practise.

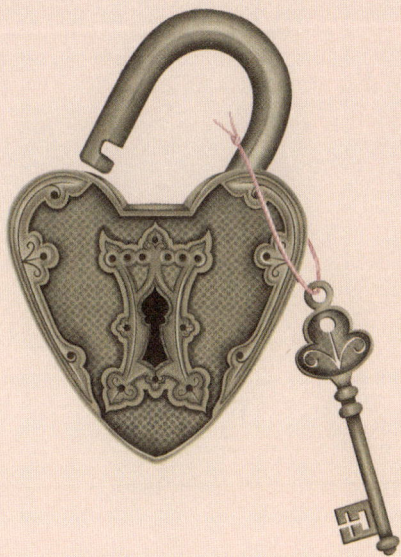

Where perfectionism is, real love cannot exist.

It's not always
that serious!
Levity heals.

Experiencing
hurt and loss
is what makes
one wise.

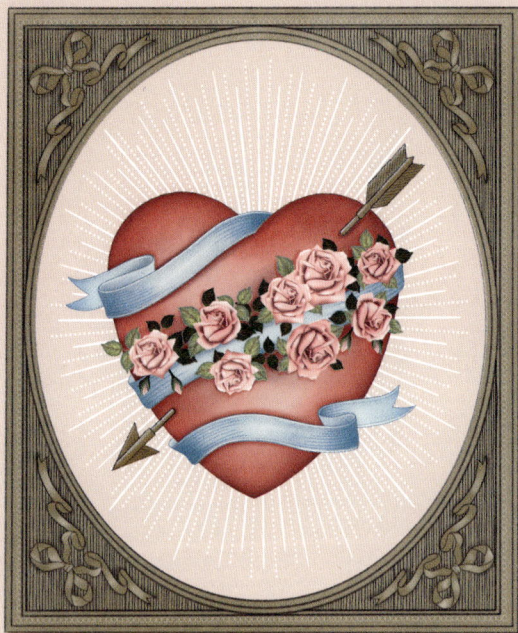

What you resist (repress, deny, etc.) will persist.

You don't have
to let your
heart die to be
a grown up.

Your understanding
of love has been
shaped by your life –
it can be reshaped too.

**Trauma lives
in the body.
So too do endless
wells of awe.**

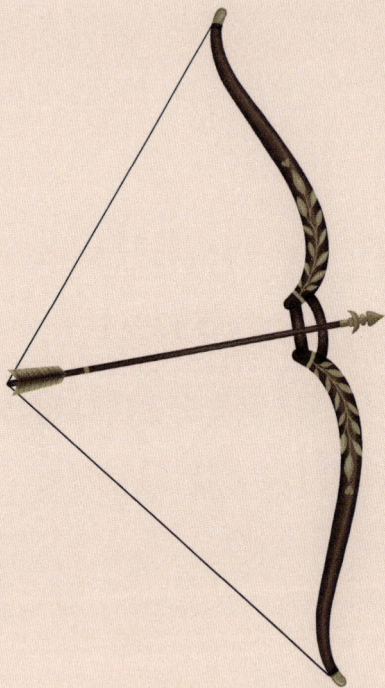

LOVE
JOYFULLY.

Make a list of 30 essential qualities you desire in a kindred seeker.

Cherish excitement more than you cherish the rules.

CUT THE ENERGETIC CORD.

You don't need
to make your
ancestors proud.
They already are.

**Cultivating
a loving gaze,
through
imagination,
transforms
the mundane.**

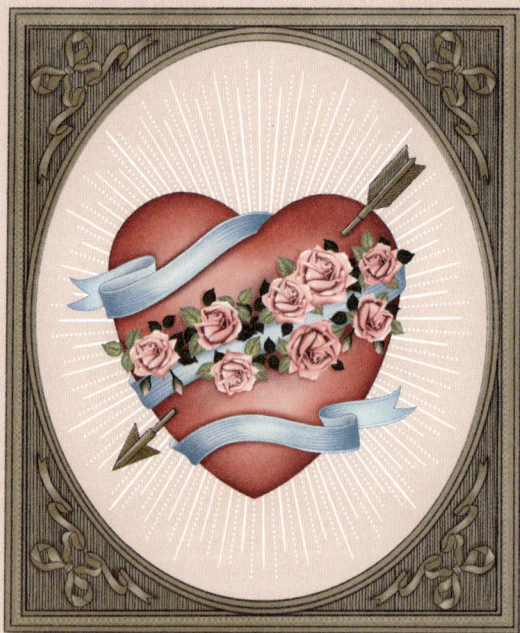

Onward,
you dashing
romantic
adventurer.

BE NOT
AFRAID!

Experience
makes
one wiser.

'If the path be beautiful, let us not question where it leads.'

ANATOLE FRANCE

What can you
do, right now, to
get a little more
conscious of love?

There is nowhere you can go that love won't find you.

Love is the rule,
not the exception.
Ignore those who
tell themselves
otherwise.

It's time to
explore the
full scope of
your erotic
landscape.

Romance is a drug. Use responsibly.

**Fantasy is
not escapism.
It's a way
to understand
yourself on
a deeper level.**

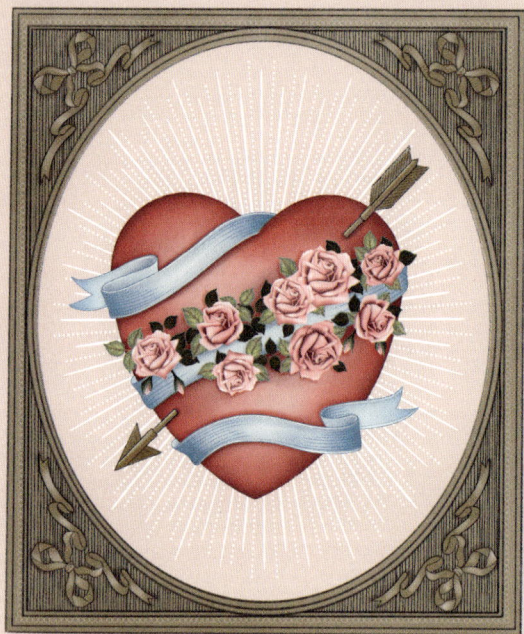

You are the
only champion
you need.

Self-surveillance isn't the same as self-love.

Don't look to another to unlock a passion only you yourself hold the key to.

Either say it, or forever hold your peace.

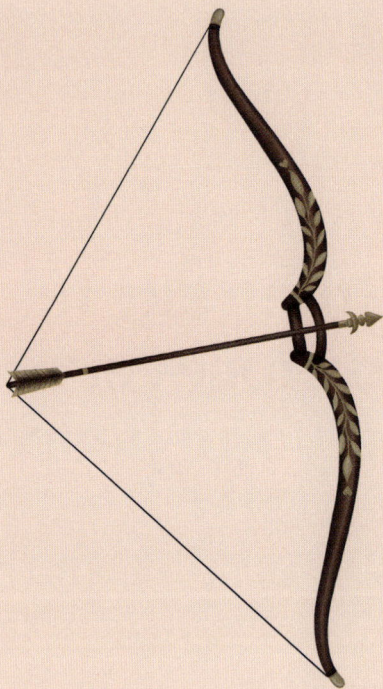

**Power
crushes spirits.
Collectivity
emboldens them.**

Our friends who love us are our lovers for life.

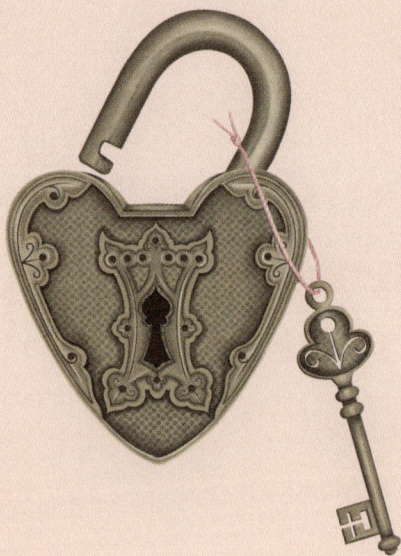

YOUNG
HEARTS,
RUN FREE.

Make a sensual cave, or refreshing oasis, of your intimate spaces.

To hold the
gaze of another
requires mutual
trust and
generosity.

Don't rush it.
Take all the
moment-to-moment
beauty in.

'No mud,
no lotus.'

THICH NHAT HANH

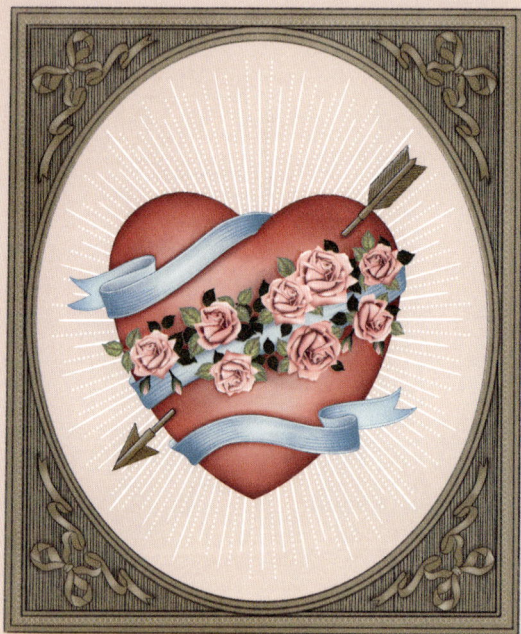

The more pleasure, the more power.

You're invited
to unpack the
structures
of oppression
seeping into
your self-image.

You can't fully process your emotions without tending to your nervous system.

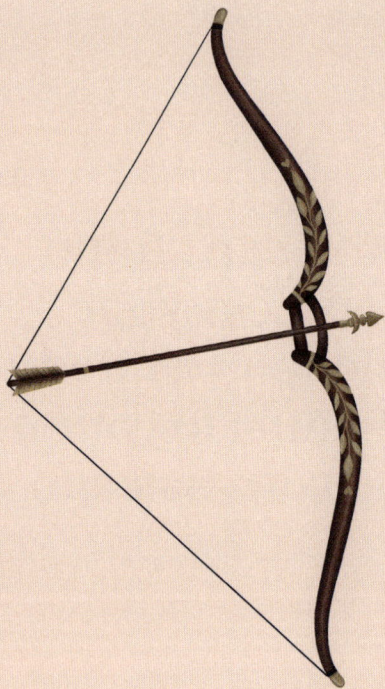

Make your life a devotional practice, inside and out.

When it comes
to sex, lead
by example:
show *and* tell.

How is your
heart trying
to protect you,
based on what
it knows?

GILD NOT THE LILY OF LOVE.

Create thoughts that affirm your agency.

Don't debate your worth. Decide on it.

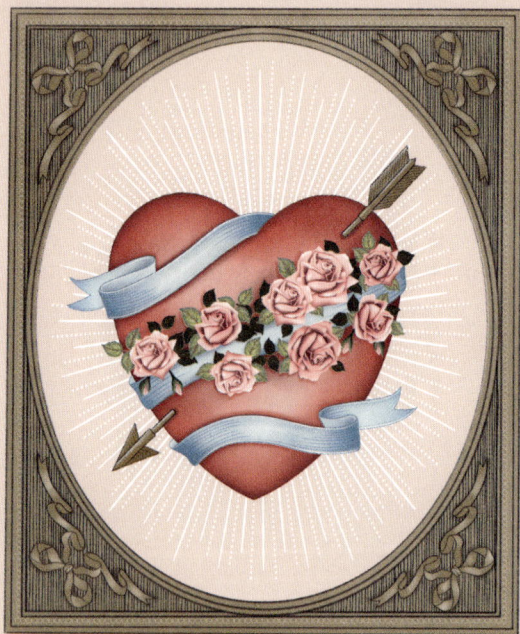

You're not
denying your
darkness when
choosing to look
up at the light.

Shame is the killer of connection.

Don't just
share what
you want –
ask what
they want.

TRUE LOVE
INCLUDES
SELF-SOVEREIGNTY.

'God is change.'

OCTAVIA BUTLER

Make a wish!
Now make
a plan.

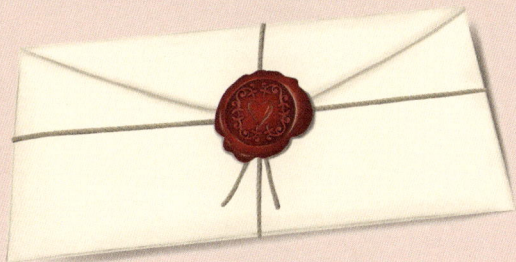

There is nothing
more brave
or more true than
sharing your heart
with another.

Love should
always *restore*
your energy.
Not drain it.

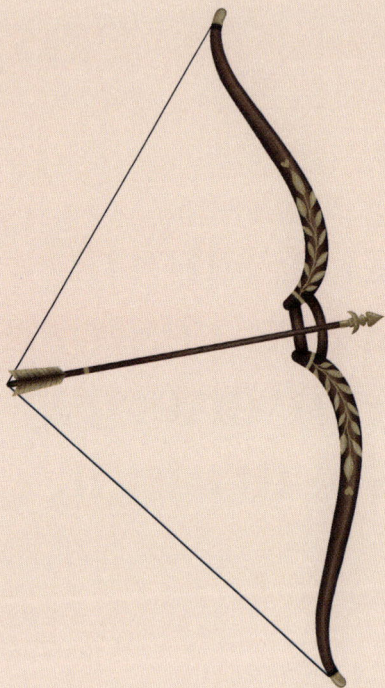

Practise radical aliveness, the state of living from the heart.

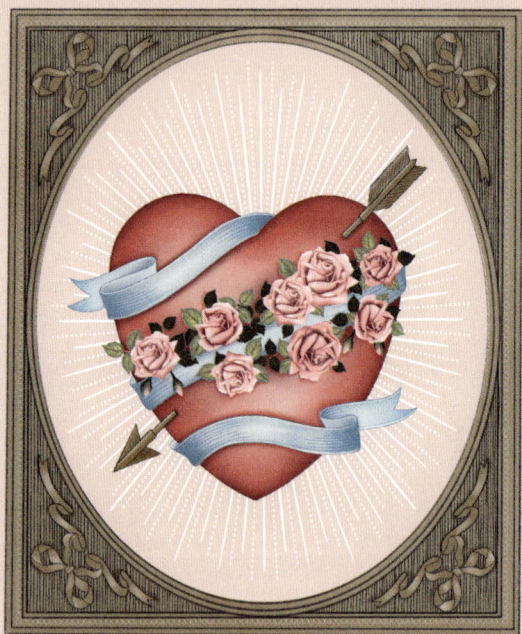

YOU ONLY
LIVE ONCE.

There's so much beauty in how the unfolding of time marks you.

Love demands that we erase all imagined hierarchy, from our mind and the world.

We *all* have
the capacity to
be toxic. No one
is immune.

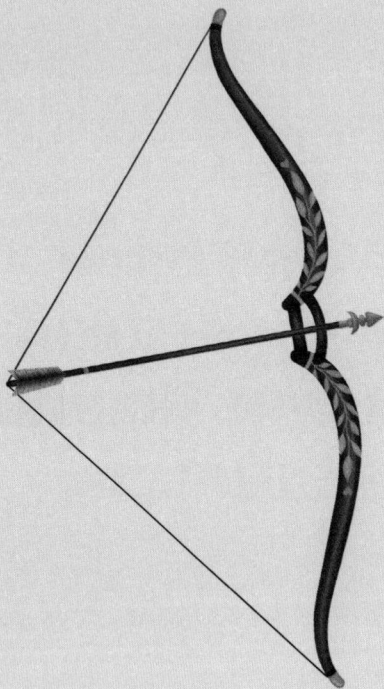

LOVE IS
A DAILY
DISCIPLINE.

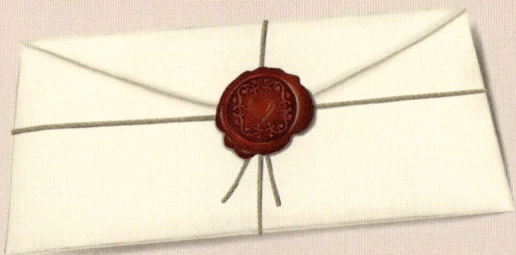

For each fearful
thought, add
a ridiculously
loving thought.

Don't think
too much.
What does your
heart say?

Love can't breathe when it's smothered.

Real love isn't about losing or changing yourself.

Make loving fun! Enjoyment is the glue of all relationships.

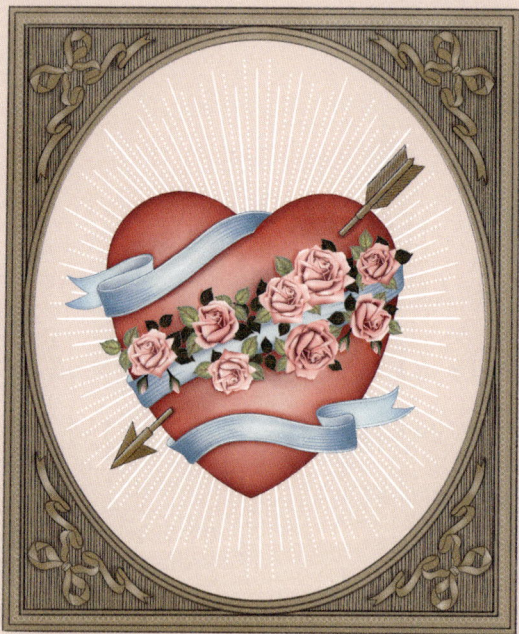

Love is patient.
Can *you* be?

'Know thyself'
is the mystic's
greatest work
and the lover's
greatest test.

Life is a series of cycles – every season has its purpose.

Empowerment is the engine of great sex.

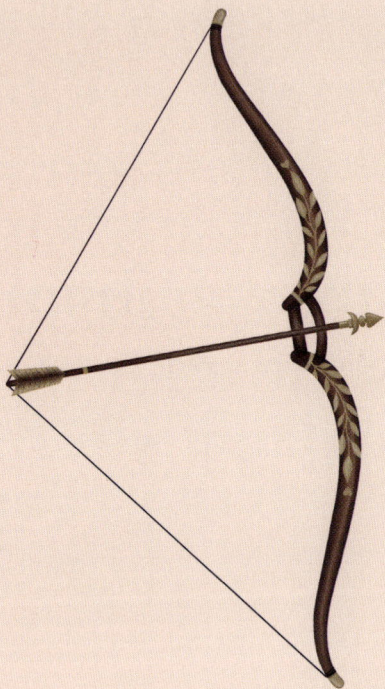

What if love was the only thing that exists?

What turns you on? Make an extensive list.

The way we
treat ourselves
is the way we teach
others to treat us.

HOLD IT
LIGHTLY.

Every day,
in every way,
orient yourself
towards
goodness.

It takes two to tango. Relationality is a dance.

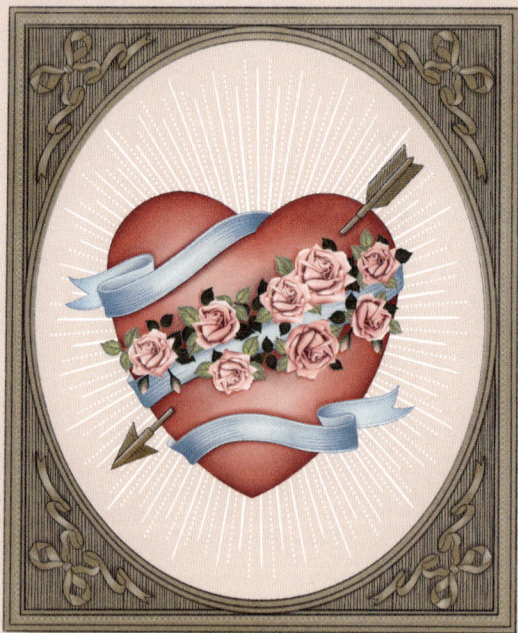

Come home
to your heart.
You already have
the answers.

**To feel pain
is to know
you're ALIVE.**

Be defiant and
bold in your
vulnerability.

What does a kindred spirit look like?

Give your inner child permission to love things unabashedly.

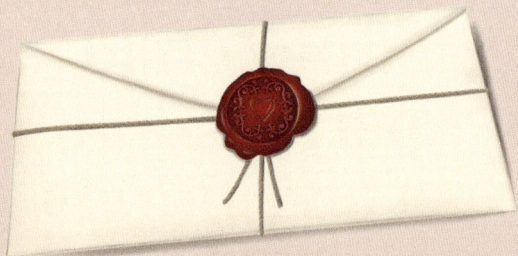

Live like poetry. Make art of your life.

'Love is
an action.
Never simply
a feeling.'

BELL HOOKS

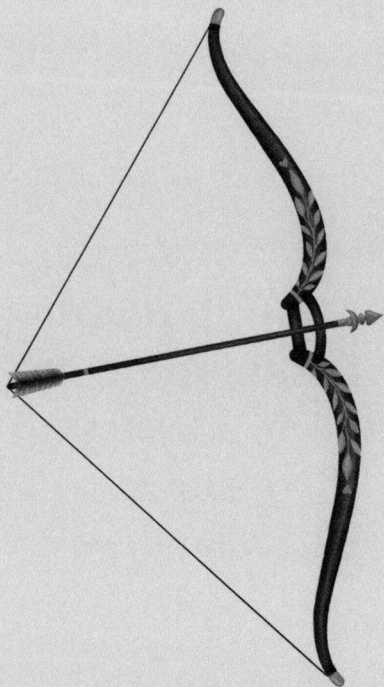

Stop everything.
Stand in front
of your mirror
and say 'I love you'
20 times.

Yesterday was heavy. Put it down.

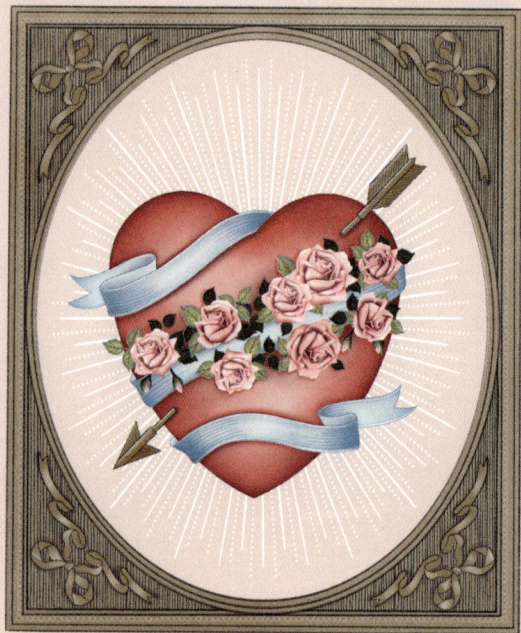

When you shuffle off
this mortal coil, love
is the sole thing you
can take with you.

It's love that
connects you
to every other
living thing.

The best, most essential things are always free.

Are you
manifesting?
Or just making
smarter choices?
Both can be magic.

How might you
let it be easy?
Think about it.

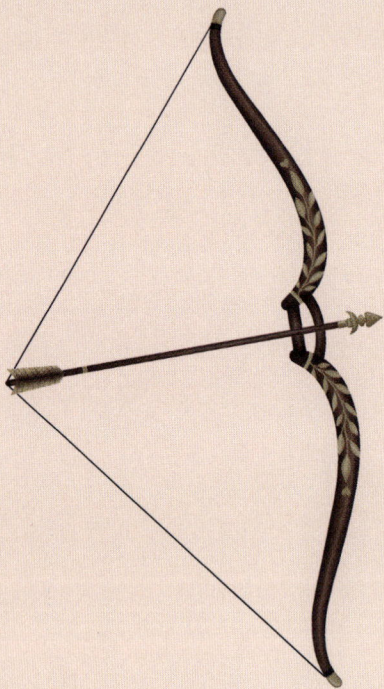

To love and to be loved. That is your birthright.

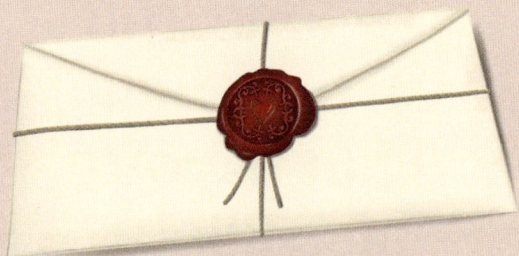

Wherever you go, be a seeker of love.

Learning to love
and trust yourself,
first, allows the
best relationships
to bloom.

You contain
multitudes.
Just like
everyone does.

Feel
apologetically.

You'll never regret a life full of 'I love you'.

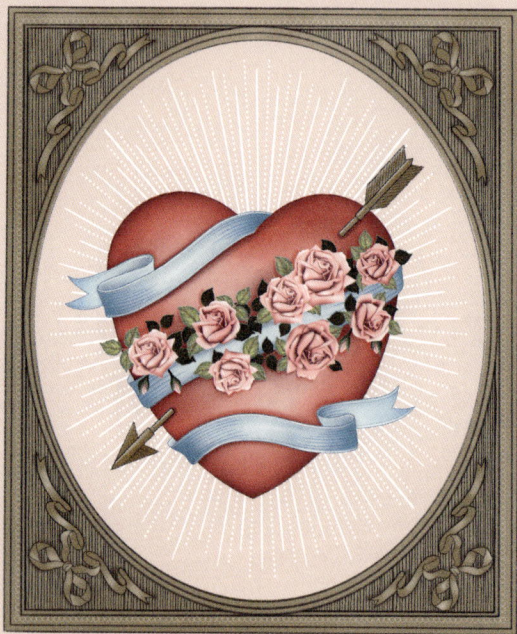

The more we
understand our
own heart, the more
we understand what
the world needs.

Ageing is a blessing and a privilege.

You're not meant
to dissolve into
another. You're
meant to grow
in parallel.

Identify your heart's
repressed parts.
And make friends
with them.

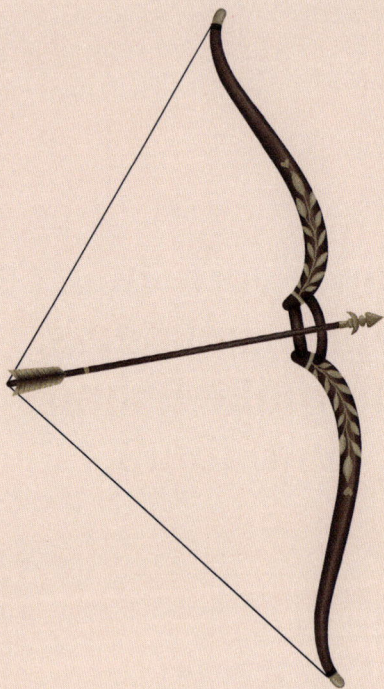

A snake sheds its skin as its growth demands. Humans are the same. We're always growing.

Don't underestimate the gift of chosen family.

Hope is fragile.
Protect it.

Breathe as if every
breath contains
all the love
in the universe.
Because it does.

You're brave enough to find out.

The only winning move is not to play.

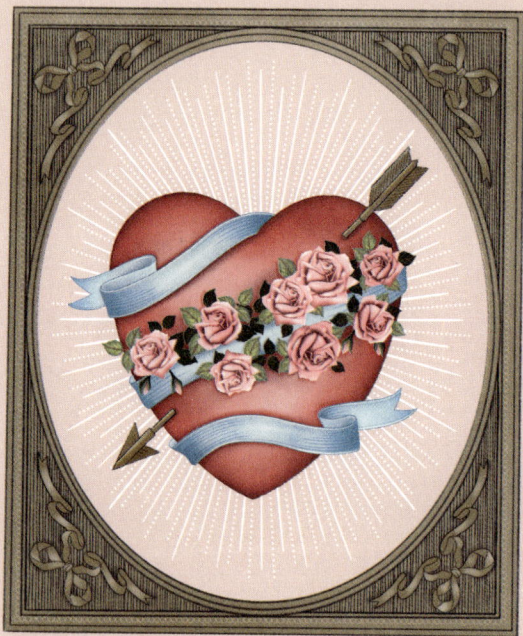

Liberate your thinking brain by fully inhabiting your body.

Don't deny your innate need for human touch.

A truly generous heart is the genesis of devotion.

Love thrives with
'set and setting'.
Surround yourself
with things that
bring you joy.

Practise aligning
your actions
with your words
– and see what
happens.

Enough about them. What do *you* want?

Peak through the veil of 'black and white' dualistic thinking.

**Speak up!
Your heart wants
to be heard.**

Love is
the art of
endurance.

'We are
born of love.
Love is
our mother.'

RUMI

**Suffering stems
from the illusion
of separation.
It's all one.**

You are fully resourced. Trust your body and your heart's wisdom.

**What are
your romantic
non-negotiables?
Write an
exhaustive list.**

Love has no respect for time.

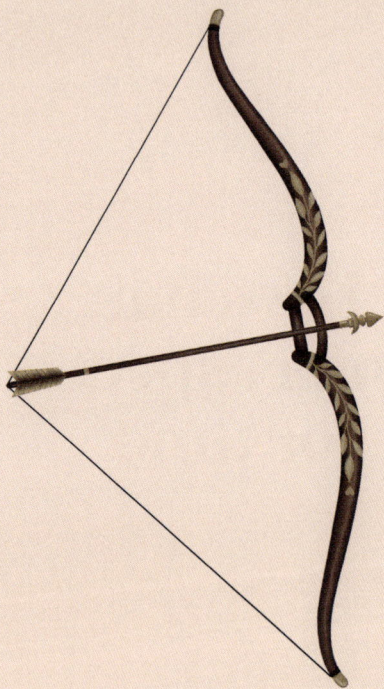

Are you holding the vision of exactly how you want to feel?

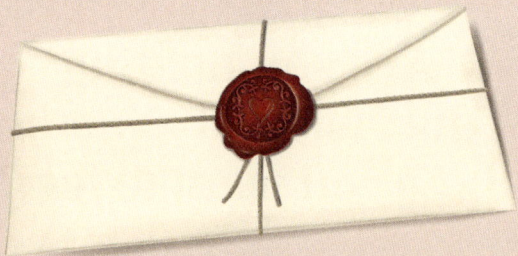

When someone tells you who they are, listen.

GIVE IT TIME.

The more you know where it comes from, the more you realise this shame is not your own. And it's not permanent.

You have a right
to feel at home
in your body.

Everybody's doing their best with what they know right now.

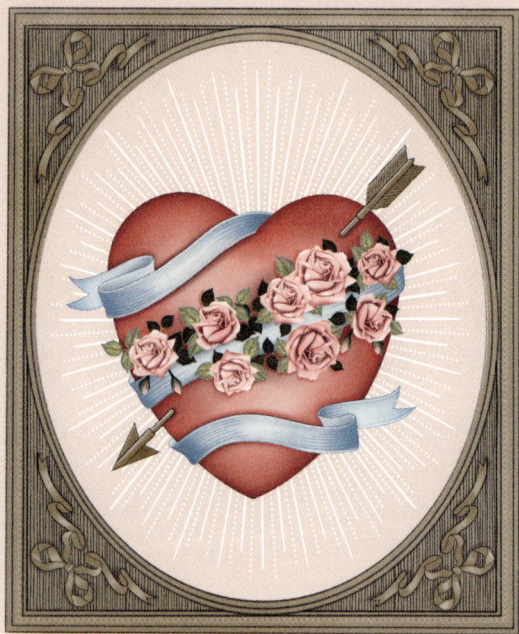

Don't look
back in anger.

What desires,
fears and drives
are you repressing
from yourself?
How can you
explore them
right now?

There is
profound ease
and emotional
fulfilment to be
found in rest.

Love doesn't shout, it whispers.

You belong to
a tapestry of love
that's so big, so
old, that it's beyond
understanding.

Autopilot is for machines. You're a human being.

Can you witness the divinity in another, mistakes and all?

Your yearning is natural. Don't be afraid of it.

Your worth cannot be measured by your performance.

What's mysterious is often what's most electrifying.

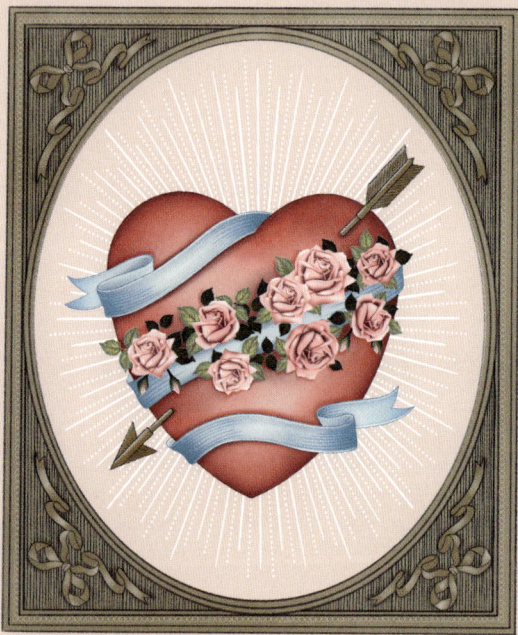

NO ONE
OWES YOU
ANYTHING.

'Love is
a friendship
set to music.'

JOSEPH CAMPBELL

We are the ones we've been waiting for. Collectively, we change the world.

Fit your own
oxygen mask
before helping
others with theirs.

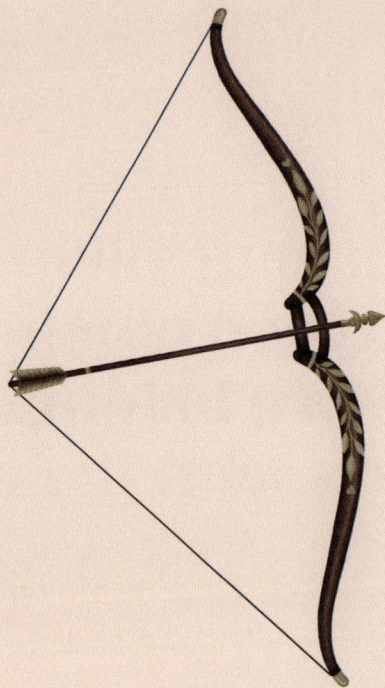

When love
hurts, that's
your heart
growing.

How can you interrogate your dualistic thinking today?

Life is a romantic adventure, even the quotidian moments.

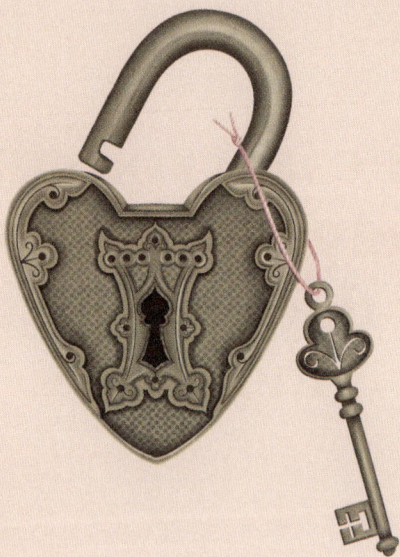

Get comfortable with being misunderstood.

They can never
take away what's
in your heart.

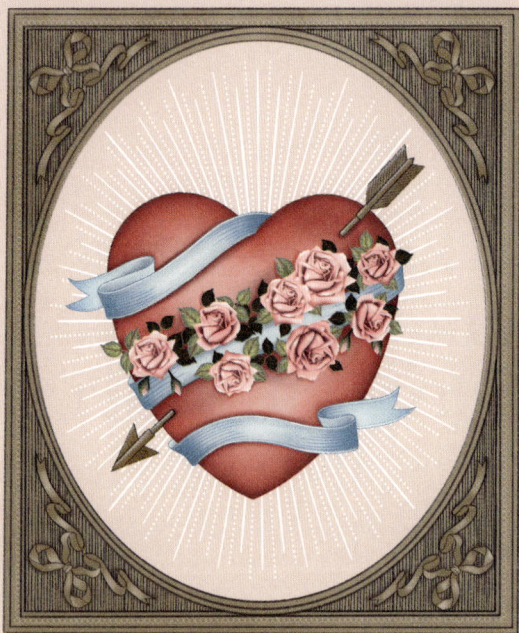

Who taught you to be ashamed of your own desire?

Love is a
choice we
make anew
everyday.

The more loving
we are to others,
the more love
we get back.

Vague daydreaming isn't enough, honey. What are the details?

Let instinct guide you in the moment.

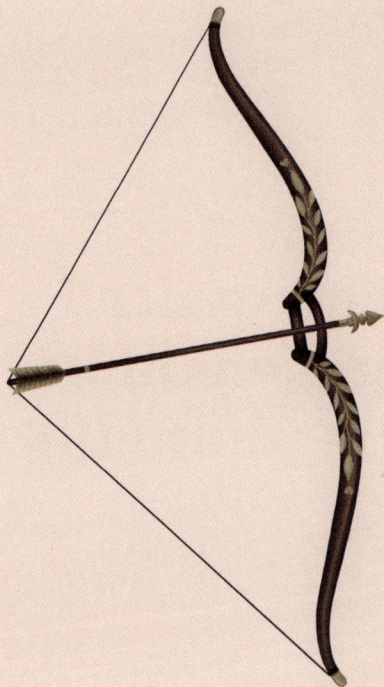

Your brain can't tell the difference between reality and imagination.

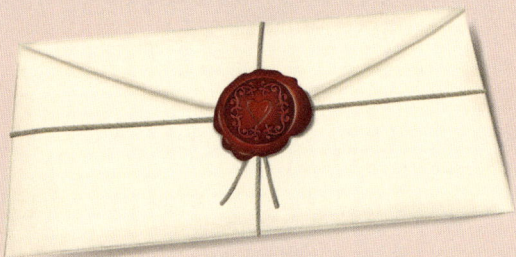

We all need space
from time to time.
Do your own thing
and let them do theirs.

Love's not a
finite resource.
It's a forever
flowing spring.

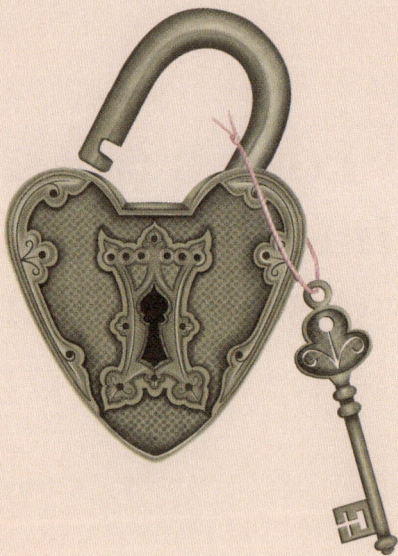

Why should our reverence be reserved for sexual partners?

Let the people you love know what they mean to you, without reservation.

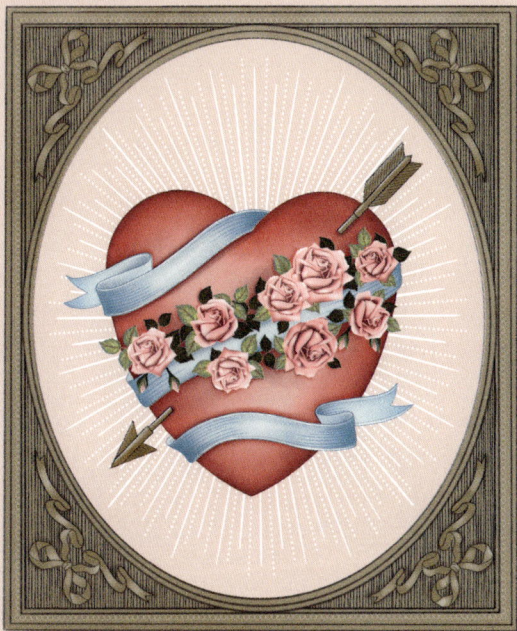

Don't wait
any longer.

**Do a body scan
and you'll see
that there is
wisdom right
here, right now.**

Acknowledgements

Warmest thanks to Coleen, Kajal, Eila, Lucy and
Claire. Thank you to my loved ones for offering
your support and care over the creation of this
book and its predecessor deck, *Please Oracle*.
Thank you to my own heart for its willingness
to crack open, again and again, to the Mystery.

Love Oracle was written on sovereign and
unceded Gadigal, Bidjigal, Birrabirragal and
Dharawal land. The author pays respects
to the Elders of this place, past and present.

About The Author

Jerico Mandybur (she/they) is an author, tarot reader, arts therapist and coach, whose work bridges the holistic and creative realms in service of individual and collective growth. Her four previous books and tarot decks – including the award-winning *Neo Tarot: A fresh approach to self-care, healing and empowerment* – have been translated into seven languages. Her work has appeared everywhere from *New York Magazine*, *VOGUE*, *LA Times*, *New York Times*, TEDx, *The Guardian*, and more.

Quadrille, Penguin Random House UK,
One Embassy Gardens, 8 Viaduct Gardens,
London SW11 7BW

Quadrille Publishing Limited is part
of the Penguin Random House group of
companies whose addresses can be found
at global.penguinrandomhouse.com

Penguin
Random House
UK

Published by Quadrille in 2025

www.penguin.co.uk

A CIP catalogue record for this book
is available from the British Library

ISBN 978-1-78488-763-6
10 9 8 7 6 5 4 3 2 1

Publishing Director: Kajal Mistry
Senior Editor: Eila Purvis
Design: Claire Warner Studio
Illustrator: Lucy Pollard
Production Controller: Martina Georgieva

Colour reproduction by p2d

Printed in China by RR Donnelley Asia
Printing Solution Limited

The authorised representative in the
EEA is Penguin Random House Ireland,
Morrison Chambers, 32 Nassau Street,
Dublin D02 YH68.

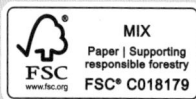

MIX
Paper | Supporting
responsible forestry
FSC
www.fsc.org
FSC® C018179